Pendulum

A Poetry Collection

Rajeshwari Nimbalkar

BookLeaf Publishing

India | USA | UK

Made with ❤ on the BookLeaf Publishing Platform
www.bookleafpub.in
www.bookleafpub.com

Dedication

To everyone who gave meaning to my life

Preface

Pendulum, for me, is more than a collection of poems—it's a mirror to the rhythm of my life. It shows how life moves: not in straight lines, but in constant motion between extremes. Each page holds a piece of me, written in moments when I felt either everything or nothing at all. Happiness and sadness, light and shadow, hope and despair—this book is built on the opposites that shaped me.

The name *Pendulum* came to me because that's exactly how my emotions have lived inside my mind—never still, always shifting. Just as a pendulum swings from side to side, my life has swayed between light and darkness, laughter and grief. These poems were born from those swings, and they are everything that I ever wanted this *Pendulum* to be like.

Each pair of poems in this book is intentionally placed to mirror that motion. The poems are paired, forming emotional contrasts. For every joyful verse, there's a darker twin—reflecting how life rarely stands still, how every high carries the shadow of a low. They contradict, clash, or complete each other—just like the phases of life they were written in. These are couple poems, bound together not just by form, but by the emotional tug-of-war they represent.

I wrote these words when I needed to feel seen by myself —when joy overflowed or sorrow silenced everything else. In sharing them, I'm letting you to see me, the real me in those moments. This is not just a book of poetry, but a timeline of emotion, a journey from the brightest corners of my mind to the places I sometimes wanted to escape from.

Many of these poems are sad because pain has a way of echoing louder, even in happiness. It often leaves a deeper mark. It lingers, sometimes even during happiness, and that's something I wanted to explore honestly. But within the sadness, I hope you also find beauty and emotions—raw, honest, and human.

Pendulum is the movement of my heart. I hope you find your own reflection somewhere in its swing.

Welcome to *Pendulum*. You're stepping into the brightest and darkest places I've ever been. Thank you for being here.

— *Rajeshwari*

Acknowledgements

To everyone who has, in any way, contributed even a little to my life, thank you. Your presence, love, and support have been the silent rhythm behind every line in this collection.

To Aai, thank you for showing me that love can exist even in the shadow of hatred, that compassion can outlive pain. You taught me that strength isn't loud, but enduring. Your courage in facing your past and your unwavering honesty helped me see myself clearly, without illusion or shame. You taught me to walk a different path, a path that I wish you had taken during many phases of your life but couldn't, to learn from the weight of your silence and your strength. I am nothing without you.

To Baba, thank you for always sacrificing your dreams and desires for my sake. You are the one who taught me resilience, compassion, and the value of words spoken from the heart, and the value of feelings that are never spoken but always have the greatest space in our hearts. You are the strongest support of my life.

To my sister—for just being there even when I tried to push you away, loving me when no one did, and encouraging me to choose myself. Also, big thanks for designing the cover of this book!

To my friends, thank you for holding space for me, for reminding me of joy, and for believing in me when I faltered. You've been the calm between the swings of the pendulum.

To my dearest friend who left me very early in this journey of life but still lives in my heart. Thank you for teaching me many life lessons in such a short interval of time and for appreciating whatever I wrote every single time I shared it with you. I miss you every day!

To the person who loved me with all my flaws and for who I am. Thank you for living the moments with me that I can cherish lifelong, for being one of the best parts of my life.

To Aaba, thank you for showing me how to love without conditions. you taught me to see the faces behind the masks and that has shaped this book. You will always be my guiding light.

This collection is as much yours as it is mine.

With love and gratitude,

Rajeshwari.

Vivacious "She"

She blazes fiercely as a burning forest,
with a lot of pain screaming from within.
Yet a smile resembling an inverted rainbow,
colorful, beautiful, and attractive of course,
she tries to put.
Transparent as water,
but her soul, turning into a black void,
ceases from knowing what blooms inside her heart.
Oh yes! Her fantasies are splintered and shattered and
shivered!
but she's still struggling to top up her desires
and to mend the small pieces of her dreams
which were missing since the day she lost her ex-self.
Like a melody everyone likes to sing,
to play on their instruments,
starves she to become a note none can play.

What a tragedy to be a woman

What a tragedy to be a woman!
If I speak for myself, a man lets me know,
how no man can stay with me.
And if I'm silent and let the injustice shatter my soul,
then a man lets me know how he can't live without me.
What a tragedy to be a woman!
When asked to stop hitting me
I'm considered rude and socially unacceptable.
And when I silently carry the scars full of shame and
disrespect,
the pride of our society is my title and label.
Oh! What a tragedy to be a woman!
My life should revolve around a man, be it a father or a
lover,
cannot be vice versa or else it would be for them,
a humiliating, sinful, and a not so manly face cover.
God! A tragedy to be a woman!
A very hard-to-love and impossible-to-understand type
of woman.
Whose love knows no boundary,
yet valuing her self-respect, dreaming about her life
is a problem and a topic to worry.

Oh my god, the tragedy to be a woman!!!
And yet wanting to be one in all the lifetimes to come.

The lioness falls

I saw the lioness fall.
And not only her body,
but her heart and soul torn into pieces and scattered,
as she looked into the eyes of her cubs watching her.
Watching her fall from a single slap,
the strongest one for them turned into a weak body
unable to defend herself.
A slap and the hero of their lives turned into the cruelest
villain.
The hands that held them so gently once,
now smacked her with so much insensitivity.
Yet she tries to rise for her cubs,
to protect their faith and love for their hero from falling
apart completely.
She stands and smiles at them.
A smile full of pain.
Pretending she wasn't hurt.
Pretending she wasn't destroyed.
Pretending she wasn't dead inside.
And pretending she wasn't full of hate,
for their hero, who was the only villain of her life.

Warm and awkward smile

Sitting across the table
I observed his grey hair.
Their count was increasing day by day.
He is old now with wrinkles on his face,
as he gives me a warm yet awkward smile.
I remember his rough and gentle hands
I used to hold while crossing the road,
hoping they still have the softness of a father's heart.
His eyes looking at me with the same feeling
when he dropped me off at school for the first time.
"Oh my sweet little girl" they say,
but not a single word comes out of his mouth.
A smile, even though a little awkward,
but rare coming from him,
made me realize that I too was maybe harsh on him.
Harsh in a way that made him guilty
for no reason as a father.
A father who never failed as Baba.
Who never let me know
what kind of heavy emotions has he gathered.
Not the old age but the burden of responsibilities
has made his back weak and bent.
But all along, all I could see
was his warm and awkward smile.

You make me happy

You make me happy!
Yes, you really do...
And trust me when I say this,
nothing can be a more heartfelt compliment than this
to a man from his woman.
Special and worthy of love
is what you make me feel,
undressing all the purest forms of my emotions.
Yes, I suck at lot of things but you!
Just being with you makes everything look easy,
don't know what magic you have in your presence,
to make me a version of myself I never imagined I could
be!
The way you make me forget the world,
ponder on you, and ruminating on all our moments is
just so mystical!
Could I ever thank you enough for pleading me
the best man I could've ever been blessed with,
for the most precious love I could've ever encountered,
and for the eternal happiness you give me,
with all the little and large things you do
for and with me?

When the weather is fine

I'll come to you like a day when the weather is fine,
even after a boisterous night.
Holding all the mystics to soothe your melancholy,
and make you heed the yearning of mine.
Melting the bergs in your heart softly,
with the warmth that wishes to soothe
the crevices of your wretched recalls eternally.
Yes, I'll come to you,
even if the storm arrives.
To silence the disquiet in your mind,
as the love I give thrives.
Thrives and bright it shines,
in the strongest of the uproars,
even when your darkest plight aligns.
I'll come to you like a day when the weather is fine,
when you can't even bear the sun above,
I'll definitely come,
just to make you shine...

That is her

She is a sculpture made by her destiny,
cause her flaws are beautiful too
and her scars read a heartening story.
A story trapped in her skin, her eyes, and in every cell of
her body!
struggling to emerge and flow.
She is not what people think of
while looking at the moon.
She strives to be the sun that burns the evil eyes.
She is the art where a lotus and fire come together,
a fine blend of enlightenment and strength
that can take over anything it wishes to.
She is the sound of waves that creep on her soul,
the petrichor that makes her attached to the earth.
She tends to be in the sky,
like an inevitable star,
you can't have and you can't stop!

Why am I?

Why am I bestirred?
Why am I full of thoughts even when I am empty inside?
Want to be vulnerable and protected at the same time...
Why am I clueless about the things I do well-planned?
These desires to be flattered but live lowkey at the same
time...
Why do I feel more vital at the time I don't even want to
exist?
Enjoying the feeling of being needed by someone,
but denying being present for them whenever they need
me.
Why am I anxious when everything is going my way
and I'm the happiest alive?
I don't know, but this is nice...
Just nice that I can't think of anything
when asked for the most regrettable thing I've done...
Maybe I've done some to have a bit of regret
But what is life if you don't slightly feel sad
for the choices you've made and still love the way
everything has turned out... Yeah?!
I also love the way this started by being awake and
ended at being satisfied...

Me, you, and life

I dream of a life.
A life that is passed with you,
holding my hand
and walking thousands of miles.
Where I have a small shelter
I call my home,
with a little pet and
having someone who will be
my eternal home, you, besides.
A life with less regrets,
and more joy.
Full of flowers that look beautiful
even when they die.
Me, you, and our radiant life,
that will be cherished
in the monochromes of time.

Me, you, and death

I don't know if I want him
to lose hope in life when I die.
Or I want him to keep on living,
and not just living, but living a bright life.
Waiting for the moment
we would reunite here, up here,
where death can no longer keep us apart.
When we will only give love
through our soul and core,
Very unentangled by
the illusion of our mere bodies.
Maybe I'll prefer to wait for him
in whichever place I go.
And see him shine bright from above.
With the faith that
he will find me even here
and hold me again
to never let me go!

Is it too much to ask for?

Not even your favorite melody
seems to rejoice in your heart.
silence is all you want.
You just see nothing but yourself,
in the dark corner of the room
left all alone,
yet the feeling is warm.
Your own body comforting you,
a peaceful night and a dawn without words,
just the time passing by,
along the chattering of birds,
living in the tree outside.
'A day with elements you want to see,
listen to, feel, and live.
Is it too much to ask for?

Nothing not correct

She was highly demanding,
cause all she wanted was an element
a man rarely gives to any woman,
his heart.
She didn't long for his body
but his soul,
which she hoped was filled with
an ardent yearning for her.
She demanded his desires,
not his choices.
She begged for reality
over the spark of love.
And she craved
an understanding look of love,
and not a lustful gaze.
And yes, there was not a single thing
which was not correct about it!

What is feels to be alive

I don't know what it means to feel alive,
but whatever it may be like,
one thing I know for sure is that,
you live because of yourself,
and that keeps you vital.
Maybe sometimes it gets a touch of influence
of the people you like and dislike, nonetheless,
you are the one who makes it worth or insignificant.
You put together all the moments
to make them either beautiful or petty.
You make it worth not regretting being content
and happy and sad and whatever you felt.
You take regrets as learnings
And success as the earnings of your journey in life.
The love you get, you cherish
And all the hate is nowhere to be seen.
And for sure, this is what aids to feel alive, maybe...

Death scares me

Death scares me.
Not in a way it does to most of them.
Not in a way that'll make everything for me unable.
Death is terrifying, unimaginable,
knowing I'd not just leave my body
But also my loved ones miserable.
It scares me to die and leave my love behind.
Leave all those things engraved in my mind.
I think love is when you think of a person
When you think of your death.
To leave that one alone in this scary world,
It is death's biggest threat.
I don't fear ceasing this life, a hell of a ride!
Not even the unpounding heart in my body.
But it frightens me to not have my mother
In my last moments, by my side.
It would shatter my heart even from above
When I see her cry.
'Life goes on,' they say, and my father weeps
Thinking that's a big lie!

I see the universe in your eyes

I see the universe
I manifest to in your eyes.
the trueness of
all the unreal wishes I've made,
in your presence, it lies.
Everything that I ever wanted,
your definition as simple as that
I have granted.
What else can I even say,
When I myself am the testimony
to the living dreams of mine
is what I'd like to call our interludes,
if I may?

I am the universe

I deleted the number
once I had learned by heart.
I saw it before deleting it,
but it was utterly unknown to me.
It felt like my heart
and brain never had learned it.
So strange and unfamiliar it seemed,
just like the person he would become
which I never imagined.
But I am glad I deleted it today,
maybe this is the first step to heal myself.
Maybe I won't see you now as I used to do it then,
no universe is visible to me in your eyes anymore.
Maybe the universe told me,
yesterday in my dreams
I myself am the universe
that fulfills my wish...

Wish to end

I wish this world ended now!
The land shattered and swallowed each one of us
as it did to Sita.
I wish there are no more screams I hear
from all the corners of this world
while sitting on my bed.
I wish I could just
stop shedding tears
when I know that
somewhere at this time
a certain 'she' is destroyed.
I wish this to end
so I won't be scared
while going out alone
and forced to be naked.
I wish this cycle of life
just stops now,
right at this moment,
so that no lives are spent
in terror and dread.

She has changed

I see her standing strong,
not needing Krishna anymore
to save her from the abhorrent crowd.
She holds the power now,
to destroy everyone who killed
her body and soul along.
I cannot spot a single speck of fear in her eyes.
I think, "No worse can occur to me than this"
is what is in her mind.
I feel the courage in her voice
fighting for that girl who faced the same fate,
and wishing she had someone
when she was silenced.
I can understand the pride she takes in being a woman
Who could never even think of such a terrible crime,
who could never exploit.
I see the Draupadi in her
who was helpless then
But can take her revenge now
with her own hands and with great strength.
Indeed, she has changed and with her
the world that claimed her weakness,
has changed...

My bright and warm friend

I had a friend who shined
and sparkled and shimmered,
And sometimes made me realize
I was worthy of it too.
She understood me when anything stupid I said.
She was more excited about my achievements
and more happy for me
when I had a pleasant day.
She was the smile that I could never forget.
A voice that my mind always wanted my ears to lend.
She knew what healed me,
The one I thought about
whenever I had to tell something to someone.
Someone I would never imagine leaving me.
But life is cruel,
it takes the best one from you very early.
But I still know you are watching me,
excited and proud and happy
for everything I am now.
Maybe the first line was wrong.
I still have a friend,
Who is with me even now!
Shining bright in the sky
as she did always.

The one I yearn to meet again,
in the next life
or in heaven if someday I go there...

I lost a friend

I am happy that I lost you
at the right time,
I think as I see our pictures
in my 'friends forever' Instagram highlight.
never did I think
I'd find a sister, a soulmate, and a friend,
in a person so distant.
That's why it's so unreal
how it all went away
in an instance.
I bet you can't see me in her,
can't share what you did with me,
and definitely can't listen to 'Sometimes its hard to be a
Woman'
in the way you did with me.
I know you will never!
"A friendship is meant to be broken and played",
maybe that explains why you left suddenly
with everything unsaid.
I still miss our conversations,
and that is the best part.
And I still wish we could have cherished it lifelong,
I still hope that in my heart.

Love has come to you

You know love has come to you
when a feeling of complete comfort finds you.
You realize butterflies are not meant to come only in the
beginning,
but in all the small moments you spend together.
Your heart doesn't need promises but understanding,
some good sense of humor to make you laugh,
and trust, that's all!
When nothing happens fast or suddenly,
wrapped in some handful of intervals,
you take time, and so does he,
to process the syncing between you.
Yes, you know when love has come to you
when actions become more valuable than confessions
and sharing the darkest of your secrets
doesn't make you anxious.
You don't need to prepare explanations,
for him to understand your thoughts.
You don't need to tell him "I understand you" to know
that you really do!
Know that LOVE has come to you
when your crazy ambitions and desires and whatnot
is not weird but special.

Weird thing about love

And yet you fall passionately every other time,
that is the weird thing about love.
The broken and toured pieces of your heart and soul
suddenly seem to be nothing.
They say 'forever is a lie'
and you know that is true
but still, you tend to gather
those shattered feelings of yours
to make them want this someone
who feels like 'THE ONE'.
You say fictional romance isn't real.
Nonetheless the same keeping you
wide awake for the whole night,
making you fantasize about fantasies.
And yes, you start doing every single thing
making you deranged for love
and yes, that is the weird thing about love.

Some people are just people

Some people are just people.
They don't have their aesthetics.
They ain't interested in likes and dislikes.
Nor do they care about the path
their life takes them on,
accepting all coming their way.
They just exist without being noticed
and with no concerns.
Some people are just people.
How it is so simple for them
to stay in the moment,
and never get wavered
even on the stormiest of nights,
or brightest of the days.
Some people are just people.
Living their lives noticing other people.
Standing in the corner and never being bothered
with the center of the stage
that could have been their
at least for a moment
Some people are just people.
Tending to give a lot
but never they receive from others.
The scarcity within them getting abundant,

yet making the roots of other trees stronger.
And me writing about them
is because I envy them the most!
Hoping Someday I'll be those
some people who are just people...

The hidden faces

It fascinates me
how we perceive different people differently.
How we cannot know
what they have suffered
through the smiles their face always shelter.
I love the way we don't have the power
to know their thoughts or their past.
So their minds can solely
be rejoiced and embarrassed.
How I see them for what they are to me
and how they see themselves in the mirror.
It fascinates me
how my brain and my heart have different opinions
for the faces they show
and the faces they hide forever.
The way they hide their misery and their sorrow,
or maybe their thoughts- evil, vulnerable, narrow, and
shallow
And I still love the fact
that happiness is what people express and share more
often
But misery is what is always hidden and alone it is
swallowed.

My poetry

I want to write poetry.
Poetry that speaks for
my sorrows and my dignity.
Telling about my broken heart
and shattered wings.
A poem that speaks for so many like me.
Picking up their nightmares
and making them an artistic dream.
Some holding swords and
some healing the long left wounds.
Some embracing me and some my screams.
I promise to pick more sorrows
to see, feel, and create the art in me,
cause happiness doesn't even come close
to what they do to me.
And maybe that's my tragedy
but I'll always write poetry.
Sometimes for me
and sometimes for the stranger who reads it very
sincerely.
And That's the kind of poetry that created me.

When life gives you Pendulum

When life gives you pain,
I hope you don't mind and be cruel to her.
Instead, you sculpt it in a way the world would call it art
and admire.
When life gives you love,
I hope you don't take it as a given,
only loving it for the spark and happiness of love.
Instead, you love it for the reality and the sacrifice of
love.
When life gives you sorrow,
I hope you don't hate it and give your dreams up.
Instead, you embrace it and make it the first step
for the best part that is yet to come.
When life gives you happiness,
I hope you don't feel like it is nothing and move
forward.
Instead, you cherish it for your life and tell your story to
your children.
When life gives you life,
I hope you live it to the fullest and ask for one more.
This time not living in life's way but making it yours.
Take it to the most beautiful and your shore.
When life gives you a pendulum,

I hope you keep on swinging it for it to remain in
motion.
Instead of resting,
may it show you the darkest and the brightest phases
and keep this cycle perpetual.

www.ingramcontent.com/pod-product-compliance
Lightning Source LLC
Chambersburg PA
CBHW051135160726
47997CB00019B/2531